❖

"Every canvas is a journey all its own."

Helen Frankenthaler

WILLIAM J. GLACKENS. *Summer House, Bayshore.* c.1910. Oil on canvas, 12 1/4″ x 15 5/8″.
Bayly Art Museum of the University of Virginia, Charlottesville.

COME
LOOK WITH ME

Exploring Landscape Art with Children

Gladys S. Blizzard

Lickle Publishing Inc • New York

This book is dedicated to my family—
together we have looked at landscapes around the world

Published by Lickle Publishing Inc

Any inquiries should be directed to Lickle Publishing Inc
590 Madison Avenue, 26th floor
New York, NY 10022
[212] 371 5444

Library of Congress
Cataloging–in–Publication Data

Blizzard, Gladys S.
        Come look with me: exploring landscape art with children / Gladys
S. Blizzard
                p.   cm.
        Summary: Presents twelve color reproductions of landscape paintings
by such artists as Vincent van Gogh, M.C. Escher, and Georgia O'Keefe,
with questions to stimulate discussion and background information on each
artist and painting.
        ISBN 0-934738-95-5
                1. Landscape painting—Juvenile literature. 2. Painting—Appreciation
—Juvenile literature.   [1. Landscape painting. 2. Art
appreciation.]   I. Title
ND 1340.B55   1991
758'.1—dc20   91–34320
                                                                              CIP
                                                                              AC

LICKLE PUBLISHING INC

Contents

Preface

How often in our daily lives do we really look at our surroundings? Unlike most of us, landscape artists take the time not only to look, but also through their paintings to share with others their very special ways of seeing the world. Sometimes they paint a scene in a realistic manner, and sometimes they transform what they have seen into something else altogether. Always their visions are as individual as the artists themselves.

Observant youngsters will notice that as the world's landscapes have changed, so have those on canvas. Though some of these changes are evident in COME LOOK WITH ME: *Exploring Landscape Art with Children*, this book is not meant to be a historical survey. Its main purpose is to present boys and girls with a variety of artists and styles and to help them discover for themselves the ageless pleasure great art provides. Perhaps by examining the different ways these artists have portrayed the world around them, young people might also become more sensitive to their own surroundings.

How to use this book

COME LOOK WITH ME: *Exploring Landscape Art with Children* is the second in the COME LOOK WITH ME series of art appreciation books for youngsters. As with the first, this volume is meant to be shared with a single child or a small group.

Through years of experience, I have found that open discussions of art with children bring not only new insights but also the joy of shared experience. The aim of this book is to inspire a vigorous exchange of everyone's ideas.

The background information that accompanies each illustration can be read silently, read aloud, or paraphrased while the children look at the reproductions. To keep things lively, it's probably most effective to discuss only two or three works at a time. Ask each child to point to a part of the painting while he or she talks about it. If you are sharing with a group, be sure to ask if anyone has a different opinion. Since answers to questions about art are found in the art itself and in our perceptions of it, a number of responses are possible, and very few of them will ever be "wrong."

All the pictures in COME LOOK WITH ME are by artists whose work can be found in many books as well as in museums around the world. While there is no substitute for seeing the colors, brush strokes, and scale of an original painting, this book and others in the series can help children learn how to look at original works of art with greater understanding.

Together, children and adults can become involved in paintings through investigative looking and thinking. This helps art come alive, so that it lives in our memories. My hope is that when the children who enjoy this book encounter other works by the same artists, it will be with the happy recognition of meeting old friends.

PIETER BRUEGEL THE ELDER. *Hunters in the Snow.* 1565. Tempera on panel, 46″ x 63 3/4″.
Kunsthistorisches Museum, Vienna.

What are some of the different ways the artist shows us that this is a cold winter day?

This painting has a sense of quiet stillness about it, but the artist also shows some things that are moving. Can you name them?

The fact that some things in this painting seem near and some things seem far away gives the painting a feeling of depth. How does the artist show that some things are far away?

If you could visit this scene, where would you most like to be in the painting? Why?

Pieter Bruegel was one of the first artists to paint landscapes as his main subject rather than as a background for portraits or events. In his paintings, he shows men and women relating to their surroundings in a way which fore-shadows modern landscape painting.

In *Hunters in the Snow*, one in a series of paintings that describes the months of the year, the viewer looks down upon a silent winter scene of ordinary men and women at work and play. At the left, several people busily make a fire, and hunters, cold and weary, return home with their dogs. In contrast, children and adults enjoy themselves on the ice below.

Our eyes move from the large figures and trees in the foreground to the rugged mountains on the horizon. We can't see the faces of the people, but from the way they walk, stand, or play we can guess how each might feel about what he or she is doing. The strength and dignity of the figures come from the contrast of their gently rounded, dark silhouettes against the lighter colors of the snowy landscape.

GEORGE INNESS. *The Lackawanna Valley.* 1855. Oil on canvas, 33 7/8″ x 50 1/4″.
National Gallery of Art, Washington, D.C., Gift of Mrs. Huttleston Rogers, 1945.

If you hiked from where the boy is resting to the mountains, would it take long to get there? What route would you choose? Why? What sounds do you think you might hear along the way?

Would the painting be just as interesting without the boy? To help make up your mind, block him out with your finger. How does that change the way the painting looks?

Find an area where all the trees have been cut down and only the stumps remain. Why do you think the trees were cut? What clues does the artist give to help you decide?

As a boy growing up in New York State, George Inness once saw a man painting in a field. From that day, he knew he wanted to be an artist. Though he had some training, he was mainly self-taught and traveled through the countryside painting peaceful scenes which included cleared fields, new buildings, and other signs of settlement.

This painting was commissioned by the president of the Delaware, Lackawanna, and Western Railroad in 1855 as an advertisement for a new railway that ran through Pennsylvania. Inness was asked to paint the train, the tracks, the repair shop, and the roundhouse—a circular building where steam engines were housed and turned around.

The artist rode a stagecoach to the site, sketched it in watercolor, and returned to his studio to work in oils. In the finished painting, Inness combines accurate details and his own strong impression of the scene. The soft, even light across the landscape shows as much attention to the atmosphere and the land as to the progress represented by the railway. The rising smoke from the chimneys in the town foretells the industrialization of the country.

ALBERT BIERSTADT. *The Oregon Trail.* 1869. Oil on canvas, 31″ x 49″.
The Butler Institute of American Art, Youngstown, Ohio.

What time of day does this painting show? What clues does the artist give to help you decide?

List three words that describe the sky in this painting.

Does this look like a good place for travelers to stop? Why?

A magnifying glass or even a simple tube can help our eyes focus on the details in a painting. Try making a tube by curling your fingers and look through them to view different areas of the painting. Which area do you like best? Why?

According to most accounts, Albert Bierstadt showed little artistic promise in his youth. Still, he traveled to Europe, determined to gain the skills he needed. After four years of hard work, he returned to the United States, exhibited his paintings, and began to sell them.

By the time Bierstadt first visited the American West in 1859, Easterners were eager for pictures of the rugged territory so acclaimed by writers, miners, and surveyors. Making the most of this curiosity and the strong national pride of the time, Bierstadt painted panoramic landscapes full of light, romantic scenes of wilderness barely touched by man. For several years he enjoyed fame and fortune, but when critics found fault with his work and called it showy, his paintings decreased in popularity and price.

In *The Oregon Trail*, the sun's golden glow highlights pioneers and their horses, sheep, and cattle as they stop for water after a long day's journey. A cattle skull and bones are scattered in the foreground. Indians have set up camp in the distance. In Bierstadt's time, thousands of people made the hazardous six-month journey by horse and covered wagon along the 2,000-mile overland route from Missouri to the Pacific Northwest.

VINCENT VAN GOGH. *The Starry Night.* 1889. Oil on canvas, 29″ x 36 1/4″.
The Museum of Modern Art, New York, Acquired through the Lillie P. Bliss Bequest.

Do you think this scene looks warm or cold? Why?

What kind of mood or feeling do you have when you look at this painting? What has the artist done to give you this feeling?

Which area of the painting seems most quiet? Why?
Which area seems most active? Why?

Pretend that you have a paint brush in your hand and show how you think the artist painted the sky. How would you paint the sky in your own painting?

Vincent van Gogh was the son of a Dutch minister. He tried a number of careers, including the ministry, until at the age of 27 he decided to become a painter. Through art he expressed his compassion for mankind and his strong emotional response to the world around him. Van Gogh often included drawings in the letters he wrote nearly every day because he believed that pictures were easier to understand than words.

Today, van Gogh's paintings are some of the world's most valued works of art, but during his lifetime he sold only one. In fact, he was so poor that he sometimes went without food so that he would have enough money to buy paint.

By exaggerating shapes and colors to express his thoughts and feelings, van Gogh makes us look at our world a little differently. In *The Starry Night*, he applied his oil paint thickly in bold, swirling strokes, giving a sense of movement to the sky. The trees are painted in strong, upward motions which connect the horizontal areas of land and sky and focus our attention on the stars and clouds above. The shorter, more orderly brush strokes used for the town suggest a quiet, peaceful place.

HENRI ROUSSEAU. *The Repast of the Lion*. c.1907. Oil on canvas, 44 3/4" x 63".
The Metropolitan Museum of Art, New York, Bequest of Sam A. Lewisohn, 1951.

Do you think it would be difficult to walk in this jungle? Why?
What would you need to take with you?

Point to the lightest green. Point to the darkest green.
How many different shades of green can you find?
Why do you think the artist used so many?

The flowers and bananas in this painting are larger than they'd be
in real life. Why do you think the artist painted them this way?

This painting shows things that are beautiful and a little scary at
the same time. Can you think of some other things that have both
of these qualities?

When he was 40 years old, Henri Rousseau decided to quit his job as
a toll collector in Paris and spend all of his time painting. At first, people
didn't like his work and made fun of it, calling it childlike and primitive,
but Rousseau had a style of his own and stayed with it. He wrote plays,
tried to start an art school, and took a number of different jobs to support
his painting. Eventually, other artists recognized his distinctive style and
its place in twentieth-century art.

Rousseau frequently visited the zoo and botanical gardens in Paris to
study exotic plants and animals. After gaining a basic knowledge of the
wildlife, he used his imagination to create his own jungle landscapes.

This jungle scene is more orderly than a real jungle would be. The animals are framed by tidy plants and grasses and carefully spaced trees. The
bright yellow bananas and boldly colored flowers are larger than life, lending a mysterious and lively feeling to the painting.

WILLIAM J. GLACKENS. *Summer House, Bayshore.* c.1910. Oil on canvas, 12 1/4" x 15 5/8".
Bayly Art Museum of the University of Virginia, Charlottesville.

What clues does the artist give to tell you that this is a summer scene?

If you lived in this neighborhood, what things could you do for fun?

How would you describe the leaves above the building at the left in the painting?

Look closely at the brush strokes. Find a place where they all go in one direction. Find a place where they go in different directions. Why do you think the artist painted them in different ways?

Before the days of newspaper photography, William Glackens worked as a newspaper sketch artist. He witnessed events firsthand and drew very rapidly to show others what he saw. Glackens later went to New York to work with a group of other artists who, like him, had turned away from painting the traditional landscapes, portraits, and historic scenes that were popular at the time.

These artists thought that American art should more accurately reflect American life. They painted everyday subjects—ordinary beaches, houses, and yards—even the trash cans in alleys. Soon they became known as the "Ash Can School." Their pioneering work made it easier for later American artists to paint whatever they wished.

In *Summer House, Bayshore,* Glackens shows the backyards of a row of houses crowded along the water's edge. His brilliant colors convey the happiness he saw around him; his freely placed brush strokes also suggest a playful delight in his subject. All express his enjoyment of paint for its own sake.

M. C. ESCHER. *Day and Night.* 1938. Woodcut, 15 3/8" x 26 5/8".
Philadelphia Museum of Art, Gift of Mrs. Herbert C. Morris.

Where would you have to be to get this view of a landscape?
Why?

Do you think that the birds are flying during the day or at
night? How can you tell?

Describe the landscape the birds are flying over. How is this
landscape different from the others in this book?

How many churches do you see in this picture?
How many bridges?

When M. C. Escher became interested in art at an early age, his parents
gave him his own work space in their house. He soon learned the art of
printmaking, a technique that would make the most of his creative talents.

There are a number of different methods of printmaking, and of these,
Escher specialized in woodblock prints such as *Day and Night*. Each woodcut
required a lot of planning and careful drawing. When he was satisfied with
his composition, he would sand smooth a block of very hard pear wood,
carve his design into the wood, roll it with ink, and press the design onto
paper. Though Escher was very skilled at detailed observation, he became
most famous for the creations of his own imagination. His mirror images,
complicated patterns, and logic-defying compositions were unlike the work
of anyone else.

In his symmetrical composition *Day and Night*, Escher gradually changed
the geometric shapes of the fields into the birds flying above them. The
white birds fly into night, and the black birds fly into day. Because our eyes
usually see one thing at a time while all else recedes into the background, this
picture may appear different on different viewings, depending on what you
focus on first.

STUART DAVIS. *New York Waterfront.* 1938. Gouache on paper, 12″ x 15 7/8″.
The Museum of Modern Art, New York, Given anonymously.

This is a different kind of landscape painting, called abstract. In it, the artist puts together parts of what you would see along the waterfront, both in the water and on the land. What would it be like to walk in this place?

How many colors can you find in this painting? What are they? How many circles, squares, and rectangles can you find?

Look at the various colored shapes. Point to the ones that remind you of something and tell what they remind you of.

Waterfronts are busy places. Does this place seem busy to you? Why?

Stuart Davis' career covered every major period in the development of modern American art. His parents, both artists, encouraged his interest from the beginning; at 16, he left school to study art full-time.

Davis began his career as a cartoonist and illustrator. His early art was realistic, but gradually he focused on just the parts of objects he found most intriguing. Like other abstract artists, he was more interested in color and composition than in painting something exactly the way it appears.

In *New York Waterfront*, Davis doesn't give us a factual depiction of the place. Instead, many of his shapes suggest objects that might be seen along a city harbor. The forms and colors and their organization give us the artist's impression of the scene. Davis was very interested in music, especially jazz. His paintings have been compared to jazz because of the bright colors and the broken rhythms of his playful and lively compositions.

EDWARD HOPPER. *Route 6, Eastham.* 1941. Oil on canvas, 27 1/2" x 38 1/4".
Sheldon Swope Art Museum, Terre Haute, Indiana.

What time of day do you think this painting shows?
What clues does the artist give to help you decide?

Is anything moving in this painting? If so, what?
How can you tell?

Do you think that someone lives in this house, or is it empty?
Why?

How does this painting make you feel? Why?

Edward Hopper lived most of his life in New York City. For years he supported himself working as a commercial artist and illustrator until he could afford to paint full-time. Today he is recognized as the most important realist painter of the mid-twentieth century.

Some of the artist's favorite subjects were highways, railroads, gas stations, streets, bridges, houses, and city buildings. Many of the ideas for his paintings came from his surroundings in New York; he also liked to drive along country roads in New England for inspiration.

Hopper looked closely at a scene he wanted to paint, decided what was most important, then divided his composition into simple areas void of details. Fascinated with light and shadow, he drew them as geometric shapes. These abstract effects give a feeling of stillness and loneliness to his work. The scenes he painted remind us of places we have seen—giving ordinary settings new meaning for all who look at them.

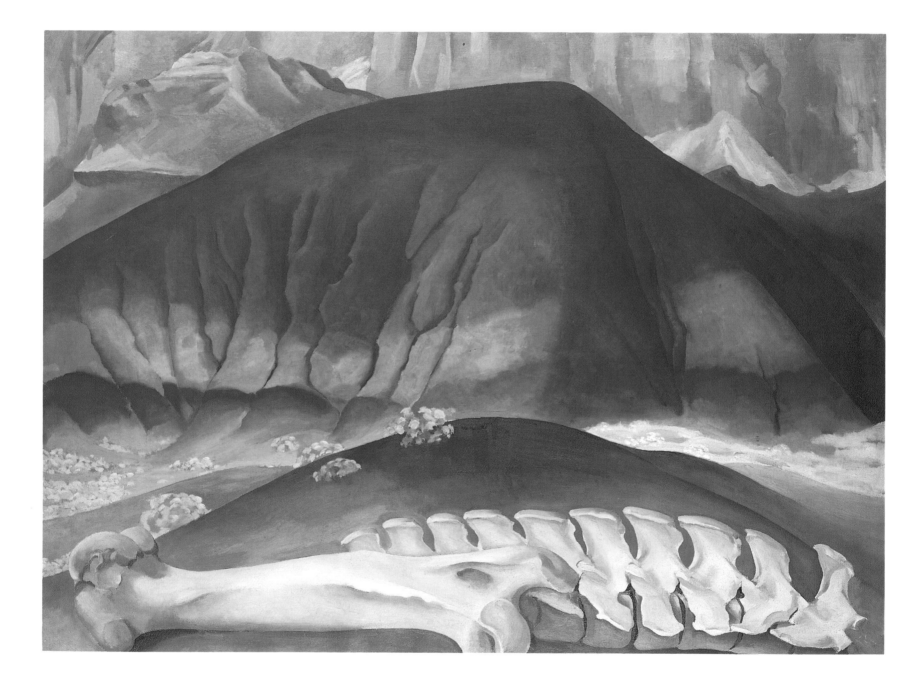

GEORGIA O'KEEFFE. *Red Hills and Bones*. 1941. Oil on canvas, 30″ x 40″.
Philadelphia Museum of Art, The Alfred Stieglitz Collection.

List three words that describe the land in this painting.

Would you like to take a walk in this place? Why?

It has been said that this painting is like a dream. What do you think? Why?

Why do you think the artist included bones in this painting? How would you compare them to the ones in Albert Bierstadt's *The Oregon Trail?*

Georgia O'Keeffe grew up on a farm in Wisconsin. As a young woman, she studied at art schools in Chicago and New York. When she taught in Texas for several years, the desert landscape of the American Southwest made a lasting impression on her.

In her later years, O'Keeffe moved to a remote area of New Mexico. The isolation and the stark beauty of the place inspired much of her work. She often climbed a ladder to sit on the roof of her simple mud-brick house to watch how the colors of the sun and clouds changed the appearance of the landscape she called "my world." O'Keeffe took long walks through the desert collecting stones and animal bones which frequently became subjects for her paintings. She used the forms of nature to express herself, and once wrote, "I found that I could say things with color and shapes that I couldn't say in any other way—things that I had no words for."

In *Red Hills and Bones*, O'Keeffe records the intense warm colors of the hills that surrounded her home. The flowering bushes scattered in the middle ground of the painting slightly soften the otherwise barren scene. The bleached bones in the foreground anchor the undulating hills, and the shapes of the bones repeat their curves. The three-dimensional effect of the bones is created with subtle shades that echo other reds in the landscape.

10/26/52

HELEN FRANKENTHALER. *Mountains and Sea.* 1952. Oil on canvas, 86 5/8" x 117 1/4".
The collection of the artist, on loan to the National Gallery of Art, Washington, D.C. ©Helen Frankenthaler 1991.

What is the first color you see in this painting?
Why do you think you notice it first?

The colors and shapes the artist used in this painting create
a kind of rhythm. Can you find a color that seems to skip?
One that seems to slide? One that seems to balloon, grow,
or expand?

Would you say that this painting is exciting, dull, quiet, sad,
or cheerful? Why?

When commenting on her painting *Mountains and Sea*,
the artist said, "The landscapes were in my arms as I did it."
What do you think she meant?

As a girl growing up in New York City, Helen Frankenthaler had out-
standing art teachers who helped shape her early career. With a thorough
background in traditional art, she began to experiment with color, form, and
technique in a very individual way. She is credited as being the first artist to
soak thinned paint into her canvas, a revolutionary technique which has
widely influenced contemporary artists.

Frankenthaler spreads untreated canvas on her studio floor, then walks
around and onto the canvas, pouring, brushing, rolling, or sponging a thin
solution of paint onto the surface, composing as she goes. The color soaks
into the canvas and stains it, enhancing the texture of the fabric. The place-
ment, shapes, and colors in Frankenthaler's paintings give a feeling of space,
light, and energy.

The artist turned the wooded peaks and the water she sketched on a trip
to Nova Scotia into the subtle, transparent, and flowing colors of *Mountains
and Sea*. Her painting is not a picture of exactly what she saw *in* nature.
Instead, her abstract forms relate to her experience *of* nature.

RICHARD ESTES. *Michigan Avenue with View of the Art Institute*. 1984. Oil on canvas, 36″ x 48″.
The Art Institute of Chicago, Gift of the Capital Campaign Fund, 1984. ©1991 The Art Institute of Chicago.

What are some of the different ways the artist shows us that this is a large city?

How many different rooftops can you see? Point to them. Point to the one you think is the oldest. Point to the one you think is the newest. What makes them look new or old?

If you were standing on this street, what noises would you hear? What clues does the artist give to help you decide?

What part of the picture is a painting of the street, and what part is a reflection in the glass? Put your hand over different areas to help you decide.
How is the half of the painting that is a reflection different from the other half?

Richard Estes studied at the Art Institute of Chicago before moving to New York City to work as an artist. Best known for his paintings of modern American landscapes, Estes is considered one of the most important photorealist painters.

Estes takes photographs to use as studies for his paintings, selecting elements from several different images and combining them to create his own versions of urban scenes. In his views of the city, streets and storefronts are almost always bright and full of sunlight. His paintings help us see the city without the usual distractions of noise, clutter, confusion, or lots of people.

By using several different photographs for the information in this painting, Estes was able to paint the surface of the window glass, the reflection on it, and what was inside the window as well. He painted the details in equal focus throughout the canvas, giving us a much clearer picture than we would have with our own eyes if we were actually on the scene.

Look at all the paintings again.

Choose the one that has your favorite colors.
Choose the one that makes you feel happiest.
Choose the one that makes you feel most frightened.
Choose the one you would most like to hike in.
Choose the one you would most like to bike in.
Choose the one you would most like to live in.

On another day, do this again. What you see, think, and feel may be different.

And then keep looking!